T0288409

Little Deeds; Big Difference

CONTENTS

Grow Produce to Help	page 4
The Golden Rule and More	page 18

NATIONAL GEOGRAPHIC
School Publishing
Hampton-Brown

Words with oa, ow

oa
ow

Look at each picture. Read the words.

Example:

c**oa**st

s**oa**p

b**oa**t

cr**ow**

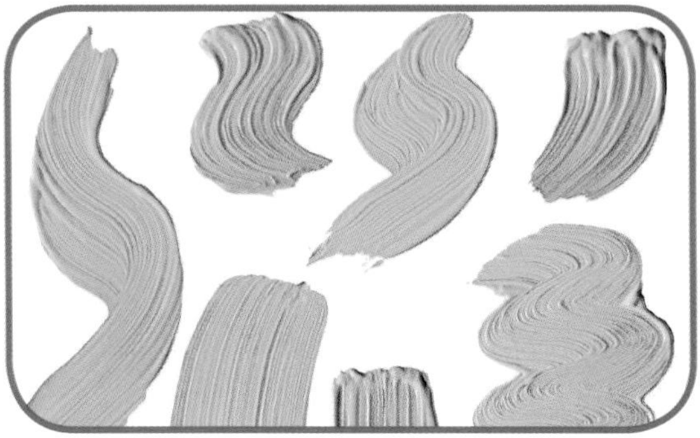

yell**ow**

wind**ow**

Key Words

Look at the pictures. Read the sentences.

High Frequency Words

- around
- ever
- may
- nice
- push
- teacher
- thank
- would

Thanks for the Food!

1. Have you **ever** grown plants to eat?
2. A **teacher** **may** help you.
3. **Push** the seeds down so they'll grow.
4. In time you'll have plants all **around**!
5. A **nice** way to help is to give some food away.
6. People **would** **thank** you for the food.

What plants would you like to grow?

GO! Phonics Games
NGReach.com

Grow Produce to Help

by Tory Wren

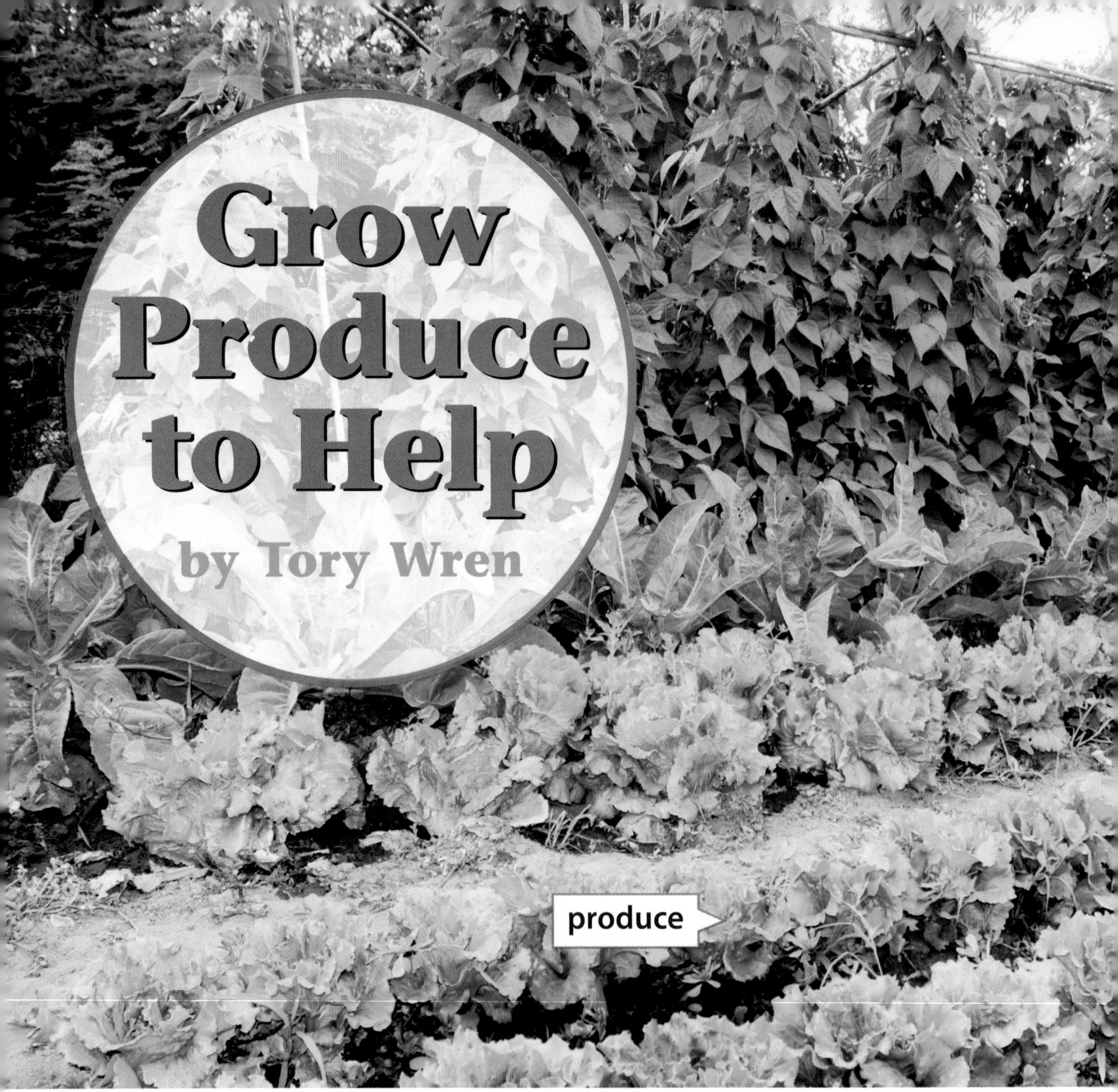

Have you ever grown a plant that you can eat? You may have grown peas or beans or kale. This is fresh produce. It's homegrown because you grow it at your home.

You don't need lots of space to grow produce. You can grow it in a pot or in a window box. It's just as good and just as fresh.

People like homegrown produce. They don't have to wait around for it to come on a boat or a plane. They can just go to their gardens and pick a load of peppers.

Think about what you can do with your homegrown produce. You can roast it or toast it. You can bake it or put it in a pie.

Fresh produce is important. You and your family can eat the produce that you grow in the garden. That can help you stay well.

But what if people don't have fresh produce to eat? What if they need more to eat? Some people like a program called Plant a Row. This is how it works.

People plant a row of beans or peas for their family. Then they plant a row to donate to a food bank. A food bank is where people can go if they need food.

Lots of classes in the United States grow their own produce. These kids are growing a garden. They will eat the fresh food and take some home.

If your class plants a garden, you will need each of these objects. Can you name them? Your teacher may need to help you push the big wheelbarrow.

Plant your garden in neat rows. Push the seeds down deep into the soil. Wait for the produce to grow.

Growing fresh produce is a big job. You must wait for it to grow. But don't give up! People will thank you for helping them eat well.

Words with oa, ow

Read these words.

boat	sow	lots	toast	loads
grow	land	plant	rows	window

Find the words with **oa** and **ow**. Use letters to build them.

b o a t

Talk Together

Choose words from the box above to tell about this picture.

Peope can sow seeds in rows.

o

More Words with Long o

Look at each picture. Read the words.

Example:

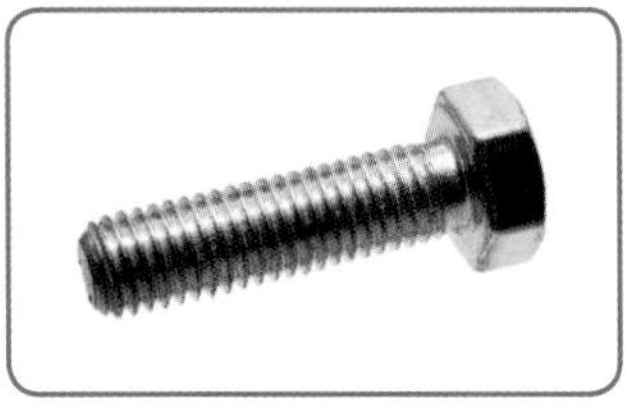

bolt

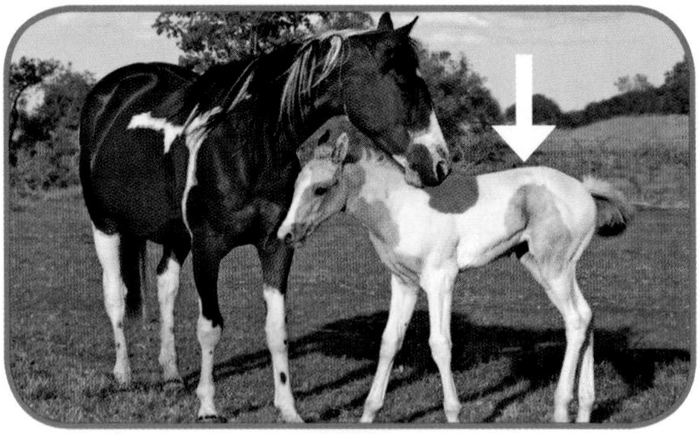

colt

post

gold

rolls

cold

High Frequency Words

- around
- ever
- may
- nice
- push
- teacher
- thank
- would

Key Words

Look at the pictures. Read the sentences.

Thank You for Helping!

1. Do you **ever** help other people?
2. It **would** be a **nice** thing to do.
3. You should be nice and not **push**.
4. You **may** help your **teacher** and friends.
5. You can do good deeds all **around**!
6. People will say, "**Thank** you!"

What is a nice way to help people?

Phonics Games

NGReach.com

The Golden Rule and More

by Janet Ward

The Golden Rule is hundreds of years old. It's an old rule and a good rule. Here it is: Treat people the way you would like them to treat you.

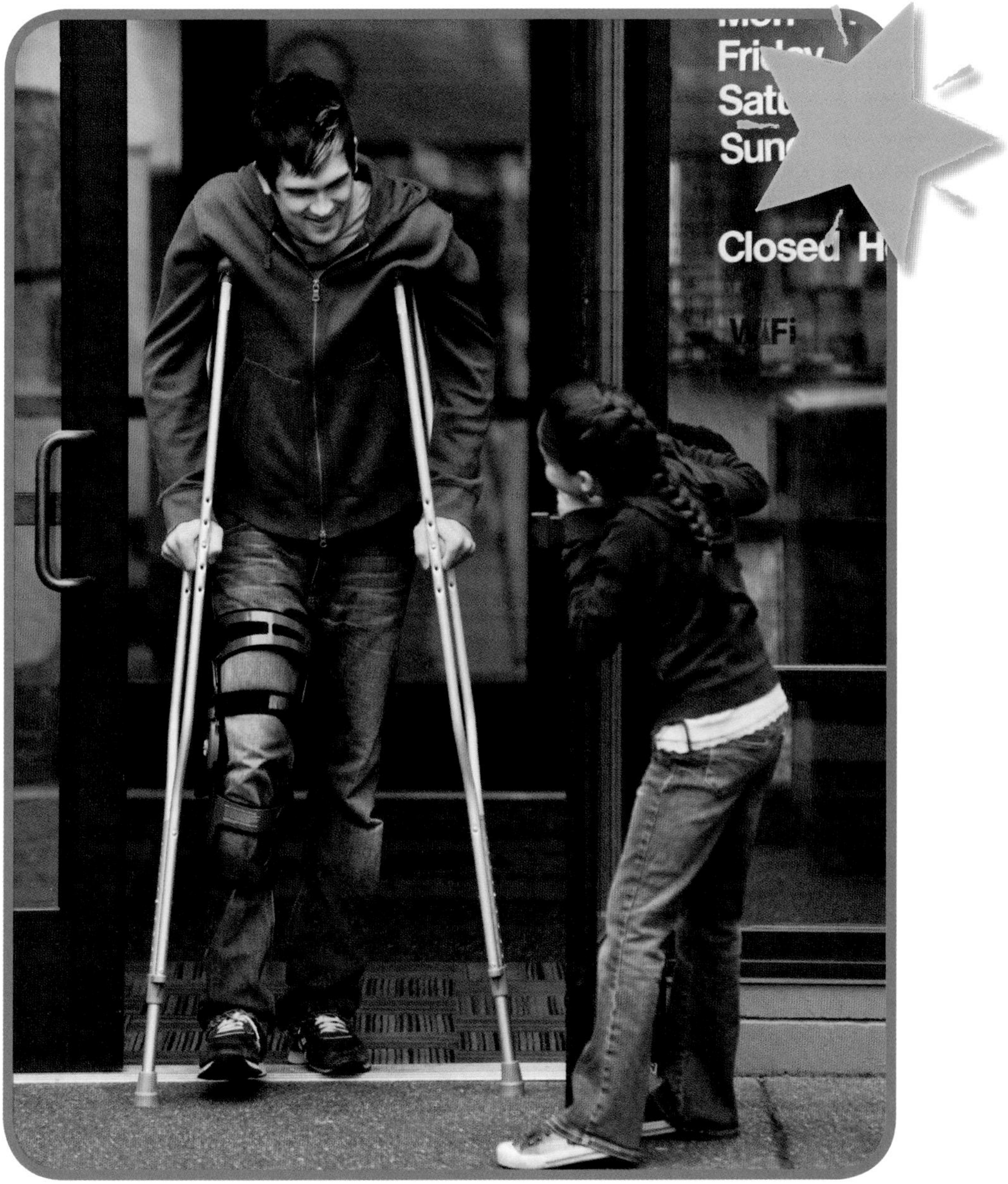

Here are people helping people. They are following the Golden Rule. You will read about some great rules to follow both at home and at school.

1. Share Your Things.

Don't throw away nice things. You may grow out of a coat. But others may need it. It may be old for you, but it can be nice for other kids.

2. Be a Big Help at Home.

You may help your mom or dad fold clothes or put them away. It's important to help around your home.

3. Be Safe at Home.

Ask grownups for help. Don't use the stove or the microwave alone. Use potholders to hold hot pots and pans.

4. Be Kind to Others.

Ask for things in a nice way. Don't boss people around. Do you like it if people are mean to you? No. So be kind to others.

5. Use Good Manners at Home.

When people give you a gift or do something nice for you, say "Thank you." That's so important.

6. Use Good Manners at School.

Be nice when you wait in line. Don't push. You wouldn't like to be pushed, would you?

7. Be Neat.

Help your teachers keep the school neat. Pick up things you drop. Toss them in the trash. Most people will thank you for it.

8. Wash Your Hands.

Don't pass a cold around. You would not want your friend to make you sick, so stay away from kids if you have a cold.

You can help to make the world a better place! Follow the Golden Rule at home and at school.

More Words with Long o

Read these words.

post	pans	fold	doors	hold
use	sheets	golden	potholders	open

Find the words with **o**.
Use letters to build them.

p o s t

Talk Together

Choose words from the box above to tell your partner what the man can do.

The man can hold pans.

The Golden Rule Game

Put a marker on START. Take turns with a partner.
Roll the dice and move your marker.

ABC
You pushed a friend. Go back 2.
Look around and find something yellow.
Your pencil is broken. Go back 1.
What is the Golden Rule?
You borrowed a yo-yo, gave it back, and said "thank you."
END

Acknowledgments
Grateful acknowledgment is given to the authors, artists, photographers, museums, publishers, and agents for permission to reprint copyrighted material. Every effort has been made to secure the appropriate permission. If any omissions have been made or if corrections are required, please contact the Publisher.

Photographic Credits
CVR Morgan Lane Photography/Alamy Images. **2** (bl) ryasick photography/Shutterstock. (br) travis manley/Shutterstock. (cl) John Foxx Images/Imagestate. (rbc) Don Mason/Jupiterimages. (rct) Big Pants Production/Shutterstock. (tl) Photodisc/Getty Images. **3** Liz Garza Williams/ Hampton-Brown/National Geographic School Publishing. **4-5** Carmen Martínez Banús/ iStockphoto. **5** (bg) Stargazer/Shutterstock. (bg) Dorling Kindersley/Getty Images. (inset) YinYang/iStockphoto. **6-7** (bg) pidjoe/iStockphoto. **7** Liza McCorkle/iStockphoto. (bg) Stargazer/Shutterstock. (inset) Kristen Johansen/iStockphoto. **8** (bg) Stargazer/Shutterstock. (l) Francisco Romero/iStockphoto. **8-9** (bg) Oote Boe Photography 3/Alamy Images. **10** (bg) Stargazer/Shutterstock. (c) Aurora Photos/Alamy Images. (t)(b) Artville. **11** Paula Solloway/ Alamy Images. **12** (bg) Stargazer/Shutterstock. (bl, c, tl, tr) Stockbyte/Getty Images. (br, cl) PhotoDisc/Getty Images. **13** LianeM/Shutterstock. **14** (bg) Stargazer/Shutterstock. (inset) Catalin Petolea/Shutterstock. **15** (b) Chris Price/iStockphoto. (t) Liz Garza Williams/Hampton-Brown/National Geographic School Publishing. **16** (bl, rcb) Artville. (br) Cultura/Corbis. (cl) PhotoDisc/Getty Images. (rct) elrphoto/iStockphoto. (tl) Aleksandrs Jermakovichs/Shutterstock. **17** (bc) Liz Garza Williams/Hampton-Brown/National Geographic School Publishing. (l) Masterfile. (r) Comstock Images/Getty Images. (tc) RandFaris/Corbis Super RF/Alamy Images. **18** UpperCut Images/Alamy Images. **19** Andersen Ross/Blend Images/Jupiterimages. 20 Jupiterimages. **21** Blend Images RF/Photolibrary. **22** Dave & Les Jacobs/Jupiterimages. **23** Jupiterimages/Getty Images. **24** PhotosIndia.com LLC/Alamy Images. **25** Matthias Tunger/ Corbis. **26** Michael Chamberlin/Shutterstock. **27** Datacraft - Sozaijiten/Alamy Images. **28** Andy Dean/iStockphoto. (cr) PhotoDisc/Getty Images. **29** Liz Garza Williams/Hampton-Brown/ National Geographic School Publishing.

Illustrator Credits
3, 29 Nancy Carlson; **30-31** Jannie Ho

The National Geographic Society
John M. Fahey, Jr., President & Chief Executive Officer
Gilbert M. Grosvenor, Chairman of the Board

Copyright © 2011 The Hampton-Brown Company, Inc., a wholly owned subsidiary of the National Geographic Society, publishing under the imprints National Geographic School Publishing and Hampton-Brown.

All rights reserved. No part of this book may be reproduced or transmitted in any form or by any means, electronic or mechanical, including photocopying, recording, or by an information storage and retrieval system, without permission in writing from the Publisher.

National Geographic and the Yellow Border are registered trademarks of the National Geographic Society.

National Geographic School Publishing
Hampton-Brown
www.NGSP.com

Printed in the USA.
RR Donnelley, Menasha, WI

ISBN:978-0-7362-8070-9

16 17 18 19
10 9 8 7 6